Bygone FRASERBURGH

by
Jim Buchan

C000246446

In 1878 the Royal National Lifeboat Institution established a station on the Sandlinks at Whitelink Bay, between Inverallochy and St Combs. The local laird, Colonel Fraser, gifted a site for a boat-shed to accommodate the first lifeboat to be stationed there, the *Robert Adamson*. She was replaced in 1889 by the *Three Brothers*, which cost £441. Nearly 35 feet long, with two masts and propelled by ten oars, she is shown on the carriage on which she was pulled across the dunes and sandy beach. 'Tipping's Wheel Plates', working like the tracks on a modern 'caterpillar' vehicle, were fitted on the big wheels to prevent them from sinking into the sand. In a synchronised operation, the men on the beach pulled on traces to launch the boat, bow-first into the water, as the crew began to row. By the time the station was closed in 1905, fifteen people had been rescued during thirteen missions.

© Jim Buchan 2002
First published in the United Kingdom, 2002,
by Stenlake Publishing Ltd.
Telephone: 01290 551122

ISBN 1 84033 217 4

The publishers regret that they cannot supply
copies of any pictures featured in this book.

From the 1880s, the burgeoning Shetland herring season, which was at its height in June, attracted drifters from the mainland ports. Herring curers, with coopers, gutters, and all the paraphernalia required to process the huge catches, migrated annually from their home bases to the specially constructed landing stages in the islands. In one week in June 1904, for example, in addition to the *St Rognvald*, which sailed with 'the usual contingent of fishworkers (about 700) for the Shetlands', eleven steamers left Fraserburgh 'with cargoes of fishcuring stock for Baltasound'. Another 'North Boat', the fully laden *St Magnus*, is shown leaving Fraserburgh bound for Baltasound. The holiday atmosphere generated by these departures was reflected in the attendance registers of schools serving the fishing families; there were many absentees bidding farewell to relatives going to work in Baltasound! Built in Sunderland in 1867, the *Plover* – the smack beyond the *St Magnus* – was the last sailing vessel to carry cargo in and out of Fraserburgh for the local firm of T. & J. Park.

ACKNOWLEDGEMENTS

I wish to acknowledge the help I have received when compiling this book. Members of the staff of the Aberdeenshire Library and Information Service have been particularly supportive, especially Gerald Moore, the Head of Heritage and Library; David Catto and Dorothy Dewar in Oldmeldrum; and all the assistants in Fraserburgh Public Library. Catherine Walker, Assistant Keeper in Aberdeen Maritime Museum and Dr David Bertie, Rex Findlay and other members of the staff in the Arbuthnot Museum, Peterhead, have also been very helpful. Elizabeth Rhodes, Helen Smith, and Bill Norrie – grandchildren of the photographer, William Norrie – Jessie McLean, Loraine Noble, Gilbert Buchan, George Macdonald, Ken Mitchell, Dennis Morrice, Wilson Stephen and Fraserburgh Heritage Centre supplied useful information and/or loaned photographs for reproduction.

The publishers would like to thank Hugh Brodie for providing the pictures on pages 8 (upper) and 30. Both publisher and author are indebted to the late James Chalmers, who lent several pictures from his collection of Fraserburgh postcards for use in this book.

FURTHER READING

The publications listed below were used by the author during his research. None of them is available from Stenlake Publishing. Those interested in finding out more are advised to contact their local bookshop or reference library.

Back issues of the *Fraserburgh Herald* in Fraserburgh Public Library
The Statistical Account of Scotland Volume XV, D. J. Withrington & I. R. Grant (ed.), 1982
The New Statistical Account of Scotland Volume XII Aberdeen, 1845
The Third Statistical Account of Scotland Volume 7 The County of Aberdeen, 1960
Bygone Buchan, Jim Buchan, 1987
Fraserburgh Past and Present, John Cranna, 1914
The Christian Watt Papers, David Fraser, 1983
Banff & Buchan An Illustrated Architectural Guide, Charles McKean, 1990
Names & Places, David Murison and Loraine Noble, 1995
Buchan, John B. Pratt, fourth edition, 1901
Steam Drifters Recalled Whitehills to St Combs, Joseph Reid, 2001

INTRODUCTION

Fraserburgh, alias The Broch and formerly Faithlie, stands on the north-east knuckle of Aberdeenshire, where the coastline turns westward and the promontory of Kinnaird Head projects into the North Sea. Alexander, 7th Fraser Laird of Philorth, made a harbour at the small seaport of Faithlie, which was created a burgh by a charter granted in 1546. His grandson, Alexander Fraser, succeeded him as Laird of Philorth in 1570. He improved the harbour and erected a church in Faithlie and is credited with building the castle at Kinnaird Head. On 1 July 1592 Faithlie was created a Burgh of Regality and a free port, which 'shall in all time coming be called the burgh and port of Fraser'. The royal charter also authorised Alexander Fraser, who was later knighted by James VI, to build a college and establish a university, equal in status to any other in Scotland. He built a college but it did not flourish. (Its brief existence, on the western outskirts of the town, is recalled by the present-day street named College Bounds). In 1613 Sir Alexander Fraser, as the superior, and 28 burghal feuars, agreed a contract as a basis of municipal administration. The Latin charter recording this agreement also described streets in the town, some of which still exist today, albeit with different names.

The population in the parish of Fraserburgh (formerly the parish of Philorth) numbered 2,215 in 1791, including about 1,000 in the town and 200 in 'the fishertown of Broadsea'. When *The Statistical Account of Scotland* was published in the 1790s charitable payments to 86 paupers amounted to about £50 annually. The parish school is described as 'an excellent school-house, with lodgings fit for accommodating the school-master and several boarders. On the front of the house is placed a good carving of Moses and the Ten Commandments, on free stone, found in the college of Fraserburgh, and said to have been intended for the altar-piece of its chapel.' The Moses panel is now built into a wall in the South Church. There were from 40 to 50 scholars, who were taught English, Latin, writing, arithmetic, bookkeeping, and navigation. Fishing was reported to be good, with 'a great part of the cod and lobsters bought up for the London market'. Seven local vessels, ranging from 50 to 100 tons, were engaged in coastal or foreign trade. A large quantity of oats, barley, meal, beans and potatoes was exported annually. Apart from shipbuilding, the only manufacture in the town was the spinning of imported Dutch flax into linen yarn, most of which was exported to be woven elsewhere. A chalybeate spring had been discovered 'on the south-east corner of the town' where a well was built and 'a neat house erected over it, for the accommodation of those that chose to drink the water'. It was said to be 'more fit for weak constitutions' than the water in the popular spa in Peterhead, but the 'Old Well' remained little more than a curio until 1904 when it gave way to the new railway station buildings.

By the time the report for *The New Statistical Account* was compiled in 1840, the parish population had increased to 3,080. Since 1807 £30,000 had been spent on harbour improvements, including the building of north, south and middle piers. The establishment of a savings bank in 1830 reflected the town's increasing prosperity, which was firmly based on maritime activities. During the annual herring fishing, which lasted from July to September, the local population increased by 1,200 due to the influx of shore-based workers and crews of boats from other ports. This fishery involved about 220 sailing drifters, including the 'strangers', and provided work for some 1,600 men and women. Eight trading vessels, from 45 to 155 tons, belonged to the port. Dried and pickled cod to the value of £2,000 and about 16,000 barrels of herrings were exported in 1835 as well as considerable quantities of wheat, oats, barley, pease, beans and potatoes. Timber, coal from England, lime, tiles, bricks, salt and goods for 30 shopkeepers in the town were the main imports. The kelp industry (burning seaweed as a source of soda and iodine) had declined but rope-making and sail-making were carried on to a small extent. In spite of the improvement in the local economy, about 80 paupers were supported by charitable funds to the extent of £150 annually. According to the Revd Cumming, 'Great attention is paid to the proper education of the young'. Some 100 pupils, including 20 to 30 girls, attended the parish school, where the teacher, with a salary of £130 per annum, taught English, Latin, Greek, French, writing, arithmetic, algebra, mathematics, geography, and navigation! About 400 pupils attended the nine 'venture' schools in the parish where self-appointed teachers charged parents a small fee.

The parish population increased from 4,447 to 9,715 between 1851 and 1901. By the end of the nineteenth century, the catching, curing and exporting of herrings had become the basis of the town's increasing prosperity. In the 1880s mechanised mass production was introduced to the town when canned herrings were produced in the Kinnaird Head Preserve Works; in later years the product range included other foodstuffs. Some twenty years later there was further diversification of the local economy when the Consolidated Pneumatic Tool Company established a factory in the town.

Sir Alexander Fraser of Cowie received the Barony of Philorth as his wife's dowry and so became the 1st Fraser laird of Philorth in 1375. Soon afterwards he restored part of an old building – Cairnbulg Castle near the Water of Philorth – as the family seat. It was altered several times until, by the mid-sixteenth century, it had been transformed into a Z-plan castle with two towers, one rectangular and the other circular, at diagonally opposite corners of a central block. In 1613 the 8th Fraser laird, the founder of Fraserburgh, was forced by financial difficulties to sell the castle. It changed hands several times and became so ruinous that, in 1782, it was partly dismantled and the reusable timber, ironwork, slates and glass sold at auction. The *Aberdeen Journal* reported that the remaining part of the building was extensively damaged when 'one of the walls was entirely beat down and a great part of the roof blown off' by a gale on Christmas Day, 1806. This view of Cairnbulg Castle appeared in the first photographically illustrated guidebook for the area, *The Howes o' Buchan*, which was published to mark the opening, on 24 April 1865, of the Fraserburgh section of the Formartine & Buchan Railway.

When Sir Alexander Fraser sold Cairnbulg Castle in 1613, it was agreed that he or his descendants would be given an opportunity to buy back the castle if the purchaser or his descendants decided to sell it. This did not happen and, in 1666, Sir Alexander's descendant, Lord Saltoun, built Philorth House about a mile inland from Cairnbulg Castle. In *Banff & Buchan An Illustrated Architectural Guide*, this new seat of the Frasers of Philorth is described as 'an L-plan house consisting of a massive crow-stepped block, with an enormous chimney and buttress at one end and two pepper-pot turreted round towers at the centre, and two similarly capped stair-towers projected at the rear'. After being extensively altered between 1874 and 1876, the house was completely destroyed by fire on 25 March 1915.

Cairnbulg estate, including the derelict castle (see facing page), was bought in 1862 by the trustees of the late William Duthie, a member of an Aberdeen family of shipbuilders and ship-owners, noted for developing trade with Australia (see lower photograph). When his grand-nephew, John Duthie, restored the castle on the original Z-plan, in 1896–97, the exterior walls were built of Corennie granite, his wife's dowry from her stone-merchant father. The castle became the seat of the Frasers of Philorth again in 1933, when it was bought, by Lord Saltoun, 11th in succession from Sir Alexander Fraser, who had been forced to sell it in 1613. In 1966, Lord Saltoun's daughter, Lady Saltoun, succeeded him. Her daughter is now the chatelaine of Cairnbulg Castle. Thomas the Rhymer's prophecy – *While a cock crows in the North, There'll be a Fraser at Philorth* – is still valid!

Two of the Duthie fleet, the *Cairnbulg* and the *Brilliant*, were built of iron in the Duthie yard in Aberdeen, the former in 1874 and the latter in 1877. Frequent visitors to Australia as part of the annual 'wool fleet', they were photographed in Sydney Harbour, flanked by two other 'wool ships', possibly in the late 1880s. The *Brilliant* was one of the smartest and best maintained vessels in the trade and was known among the shipping fraternity as 'Duthie's yacht'. The vessel in the right foreground is said to be the legendary *Cutty Sark*, which Duthie family tradition maintained had been beaten twice for speed by another of their boats, the *Ann Duthie*.

This print, from an 1818 aquatint by W. Daniell, appeared in Cranna's *Fraserburgh Past and Present*. Kinnaird Head Castle, crowned by the lantern of the lighthouse built by the Northern Lighthouse Commissioners in 1787, is now an integral part of the Museum of Scottish Lighthouses. It is flanked on the right by the Wine Tower – note the chimney, which is no longer there – and on the left by a doocot (dovecot). The latter was demolished during harbour improvements in the 1850s when the rock on which it stood was quarried to provide stones for piers at the Balaclava Basin, which was named after the victory in the Crimean War. It is generally agreed that Sir Alexander Fraser, 8th laird of Philorth, built the castle in the early 1570s. Dr Pratt, in his classic *Buchan*, says he laid the foundation on 6 March 1570, and built it 'in the form of a parallelogram'. However, in *Banff & Buchan An Illustrated Architectural Guide*, it is called 'a conundrum' and 'deeply anachronistic for 1570'!

The early history of the Wine Tower is a matter of conjecture. Different 'experts' have put its date of construction between the first half of the sixteenth century and 1606. Some have argued it was the *Wynd* Tower as it originally stood at the end of a lane. Others have claimed it was a wine store for the adjacent castle. It has also been said that, after dinner, the ladies remained in the castle while the laird and his male guests continued their postprandial drinking in the tower! Some have suggested that, for a time at least, it was used as a chapel while others maintained that it was a judgement-hall with a prison below. The original structure seems to have been three storeys high, with a room on each floor. The entrance, reached by a movable stair, was a door on the top floor, where there were seven skilfully carved stone bosses – three in the centre of the roof and one in each of the four window soffits (see facing page). The sole fireplace was on the top floor whence a turnpike stair ascended to the turf-covered roof, which may have had a parapet. A hatch in the floor of the top storey led to the middle room from which another hatch led to the ground floor.

The first marriage of the 8th Fraser laird of Philorth, his parents, grandparents, and great-grandparents are commemorated by coats of arms sculpted on three of the window bosses in the Wine Tower. One of the roof bosses bears the royal arms of Scotland while another, shown on the left, displays the arms of the Frasers of Philorth. The third roof boss, shown above, carries the *Arma Christi* featuring some of the emblems of the crucifixion – two angels pointing at a crown of thorns surrounding a heart, pierced hands and feet, nails, a hammer, and a scourge. Some have said this indicates support of Catholicism as does the carving of the Erskine family's arms and those of the Earl of Huntly on the boss in the north window. Neither was related to the 8th laird but they remained Catholics after the Reformation and the Earl of Huntly led the Counter-Reformation in Aberdeenshire. The *Arma Christi* and the presence of the arms of the Catholic nobility, together with the claim that there was a vestry on the top floor, have been cited by those who say the tower was a secret chapel for the Catholic wife of the Protestant 8th laird of Philorth. Conjecture continues but the Wine Tower remains an enigma.

This was a common scene during the sma'lin' (small line) fishing season when the lines were being repaired and baited before being shot on inshore fishing grounds and left overnight to catch white fish. Mussels were the preferred bait but were often unavailable locally and so had to be procured elsewhere; e.g. from the prolific beds in the Ythan estuary or Little Ferry, near Golspie. To eke out the mussels, the younger members of the family gathered limpets from the rocks at low tide. The womenfolk 'sheeled' the mussels and limpets, i.e. scooped them whole from their shells ready to be pushed on to the sharp-pointed hooks. Before this was done, the menfolk had to 'redd' (unravel) the lines, which had been carried home in sculls (shallow scoop-shaped baskets) after being hauled from the fishing grounds earlier in the day. When new hooks were required, the men used tippens (hairs from a horse's tail twisted together) to bind them securely to the sneeds (short lengths of rope), which were tied to the sma'lin' at regular distances apart.

Sorting Fish, Fraserburgh.

Before the fish-market was built in 1899, fishermen laid out their catch for sale on the open quay, as illustrated here. Women in the fishing communities eked out the family income by drying or smoking fish caught by their menfolk and selling or bartering them as they walked on their regular rounds to supply customers in the 'fermtouns'. They extended their rounds and also reduced the mileage they had to walk after the Great North of Scotland Railway introduced concessionary fares for them and transported their creels free of charge in the guard's van. Some fishwives patronised the daily sales in order to meet the increased demand for their fish. According to *The Christian Watt Papers*, the plaids worn by fishwives indicated their home villages. 'In Inverallochy and Cairnbulg they wore a red and black dice of different check; St Combs was blue and black; Broadsea black and white; Pittulie grey and white; Rosehearty natural and brown.'

8

The white-painted bands on the masts of two Inverness-registered (INS) sailing drifters moored at the North Breakwater, Fraserburgh, indicated that the boats had been 'engaged' by a herring curer. This common practice involved curers making arrangements with fishermen, before the season began, to fish exclusively for them at an agreed price per cran (see following page). The bargain was often sealed by a generous supply of whisky for the crew. In 1883, 61 curers were working locally and 60 of them had engaged a total of 762 boats. Disastrous seasons in 1884–1886 were caused by a glut of immature fish caught in small-meshed nets. The engagement system was blamed for this and so auction sales by fish-salesmen were introduced in 1887. Prices were so low that the fishermen went on strike and the boats remained in harbour. Rumours of possible blacklegs led to the destruction of the steering wheel in one boat, the theft of an anchor from another, and damage to the halyards in a third. Extra police were drafted in and HM Gunboat, *Firm*, with marines aboard, lay off the harbour in case there was civil disorder! The strike was called off. From 1888, no boats were 'engaged' and sales by auction continued.

There was no standardised measure for herrings during most of the nineteenth century. At one time, for example, on the East coast of Scotland and also at Castle Bay and Stornoway in the West, the unit of measurement was a cran, equivalent to 26¾ imperial gallons. At the same time, in other areas on the West coast, on the Isle of Man, and in Ireland, the unit was the mase, containing 5 'long hundreds' of 123 each. The Fishery Board eventually decreed a cran to be equivalent to 37½ gallons. As the herring industry expanded and catches increased, a new measure of the cran was adopted. No exact weight or number was specified. When the herrings were being discharged from the boats, four 'herring' baskets of ungutted fish were deemed to be a cran and so, when William Norrie photographed this scene at Fraserburgh harbour in the early 1890s, he entitled it 'A cran and a quarter'.

For most of the Victorian era, herring curers worked in temporary 'stations', as illustrated here, on land leased annually on, or adjacent to, the quays. Curers engaged the 'guttin quines' in crews of three – two gutters and a packer – with an advanced payment, known as arles, and then paid an agreed amount at the end of the season for each barrel they filled with gutted herrings. The herrings, already salted when being unloaded from the boats, were emptied into the farlans (large wooden troughs) where the gutters worked. The farlans in this station can be seen beyond the barrels on the left.

When the leasing of land for temporary curing stations was stopped in order to reduce congestion around the harbour, curers established permanent 'yards', such as this one, in various parts of the town. There was ample space for storing barrels and the farlans were arranged linearly at a better working height for the gutters. Before starting work, the latter tied cloots (pieces of cloth) round their fingers to protect them from the rough salt and the sharp, short-bladed gutting knife known locally as a futtle. Working at lightning speed, they deposited the guts in the gut coggies (containers placed among the herrings in the farlans) and without turning round, unerringly threw the herrings into the appropriate selection coggies (small tubs) strategically positioned behind them.

The number of 'selections', based on the size and condition of the herrings, varied with the season and the location of the fishing grounds. After being packed in salt which turned to brine, the 'selection' in each barrel – large, spent (a herring in poor condition after spawning), mattie (a young maiden herring with the roe not fully developed), etc. – was clearly stencilled on the lid. Fishery Officers inspected a random sample of barrels for export. When satisfied with the quality of the brine and the herrings, they stamped the barrels with the Crown Brand, a universally recognised guarantee that the contents were up to standard.

Archibald Maconochie and his brother James were barrow-boys in Lowestoft, where they peddled herrings purchased from local fishermen. After setting up as herring curers, they decided to extend their business to an area where curing would be possible before the East Anglian herring season began. In 1883 they decided to take advantage of the Fraserburgh summer herring fishery and leased a site, near Kinnaird Head Lighthouse, where they established the curing and kippering yard shown here. Queen Victoria, who was very fond of Maconochie's 'Royal' brand of kippers, granted the firm a Royal Warrant. After his brother died in 1895, Archibald expanded the business and increased the product range in factories in Lowestoft and Millwall, where Pan Yan Pickle Relish was produced. In spite of his exceptionally busy work schedule, Archibald Maconochie was MP for East Aberdeenshire from 1900 to 1906, when he played a significant role in further diversifying the local economy by helping to establish the CPT factory in Fraserburgh (see page 32).

The Maconochies realised the potential of canned foodstuffs, which could be exported in good condition to any part of the world, irrespective of climatic changes while the cans were in transit. They developed their curing and kippering yard into the Kinnaird Head Preserve Works with a chimney higher than usual to avoid dirtying the lenses of the neighbouring lighthouse. After an eighteen-month marketing campaign by James Maconochie in 1893–94, Australia became the firm's main overseas customer for canned herrings. The women, shown cleaning cans, were paid 4d per gross (144). The 'Old Bone Mill', on the south side of Bath Street, was equipped for the manufacture of cans and lids and was linked by a covered overhead passageway to the food canning department. During both World Wars, the firm produced the legendary M. & V. (Meat and Vegetables) tinned rations for servicemen. In the later period of World War II, thousands of tons of potatoes, cabbages, and onions were dehydrated and reduced to powder form to save space during transportation to troops in various war zones. Although an aircraft spotting post was established on the lighthouse tower where a warning signal could be activated, in April 1941 several employees were killed and many injured when the factory was hit by bombs. An unexploded bomb was later removed from the works and detonated in the sand dunes. After the war ended, the factory's air-raid shelters were used for the cultivation of mushrooms.

Broad Street, which runs northwards from Commerce Street to Saltoun Square, is the main street in the town. Looking to the Square from the junction with Frithside Street (left foreground), the stretch of Broad Street illustrated here follows the line of the old East Street, the *viam orientalem* in the Latin charter granted to the feuars by the town's founder in 1613. At that time Frithside Street was called the *viam aquaticam*, the 'water way', because of an aqueduct channelling water to the harbour from a marshy area on the south-west outskirts of the infant burgh . Later in the seventeenth century this lade was known as the Firth and an adjacent row of houses was called the Firthside, hence the name Frithside Street. The lade continued past the site now occupied by the Royal Hotel (right foreground) to the Middle Jetty where it drove a watermill to clear the harbour of rubbish and sludge. *Banff & Buchan An Illustrated Architectural Guide* states that the building on the corner of Frithside Street has 'real class'. With its Ionic colonnade, delicate ironwork balcony, low pitched roof with broad eaves, and chimneys in the form of urns, it is said that it must have been one of the most sophisticated small banks in Scotland when first built. It is now used as a solicitors' property showroom.

High Street, known as Back Street from the end of the eighteenth century until the 1870s, was called the *via borealis* (North Street) in the 1613 charter. It was 40 feet broad and ran from the end of East Street (now Broad Street) westward to Broadsea. This view, showing the junction with Cross Street (formerly Fishcross Street) on the right and the Old Parish Church in the distance, was photographed before 13 November 1919 when the Empire Picture Palace, on the left-hand side near the small omnibus, was completely destroyed by fire. The Empire Theatre, built on the site of the old picture house, was opened on 10 February 1922 with a concert by the Fraserburgh Choral Union, in aid of the Necessitous Children's Fund. Under the headline 'Concert In Aid of Hot Dinners', the *Fraserburgh Herald* reported that the evening had been a success. Readers were informed that 30,000 meals had been supplied since the establishment of the fund in the previous October; £190 had been spent on clothing and boots; and 280 children were being fed daily.

The Old Parish Church, on the right of this view of Saltoun Square from the south, was built in 1802–03 to replace the original Presbyterian parish church dating from 1572. The new church was opened for worship with a communion service on 19 September 1803. Erected in 1853–55 to replace the old Tolbooth, the building beyond the church cost £1,400 and housed the town hall, court room, police station, and, for a time, a market for fruit, vegetables, meat, and meal in the basement. It is described in *Banff & Buchan An Illustrated Architectural Guide* as 'a wonderfully flamboyant baroque corner building, whose arcaded flanks turn on the drum of a tall domed Corinthian rotunda at the corner, containing a statue of Lord Saltoun'. Its doors and windows were badly damaged during the Highlanders' Riot in July 1874, when fishermen from the Western Isles went on a drunken rampage but abandoned their threat to burn the building down after the arrival of a detachment of Gordon Highlanders from Aberdeen! The building on the left, dating from 1800, was formerly occupied by the North of Scotland Bank but now accommodates the social work department and the registrar's office. In the far distance, beyond the north end of Castle Street, is the tall chimney of the Kinnaird Head Preserve Works with, visible on its right, the upper part of the Mercat Cross in the middle of Saltoun Square. The cross has been dated to circa 1603 and bears the arms of the Frasers of Philorth, the lion rampant of the royal arms of Scotland, and the Scottish version of the early seventeenth century arms of the United Kingdom. It has been relocated more than once, most recently in 1997. The original shaft was replaced, in 1736, by Lord Alexander Saltoun; the granite base was added in 1845; and the coats of arms were refurbished in 1988.

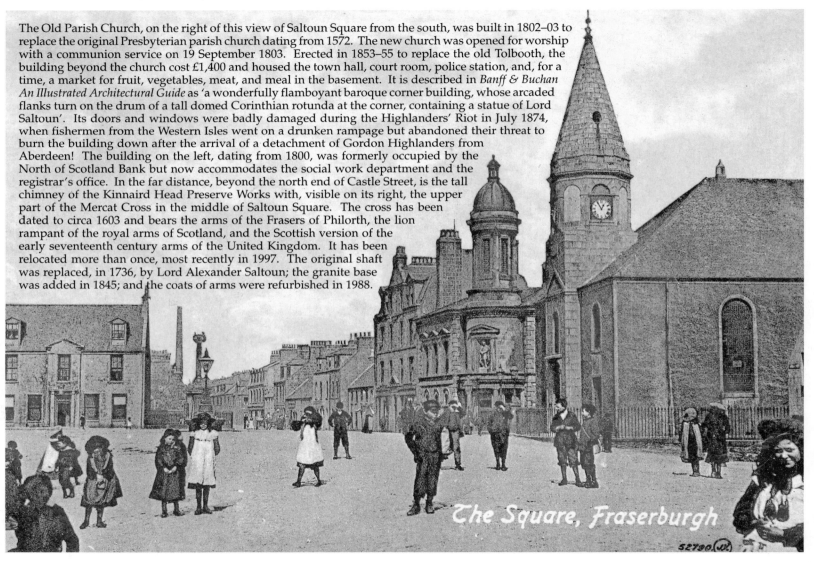

The Square, Fraserburgh

52730 (JV.)

Lord Saltoun formally opened the public library on 23 October 1905. Andrew Carnegie, the Scottish–American millionaire, had been invited to perform the ceremony but had declined because of a previous engagement. Carnegie had pledged £3,000 towards the cost of the library if the town council erected it on a rent-free site and adopted the Free Libraries Act, authorising the levying of rates for free library facilities. The Act was adopted and, with Carnegie's approval, the library was built on a site (offered by Lord Saltoun at a nominal rent) at the north end of King Edward Street. It cost between £3,400 and £3,500. The *Fraserburgh Herald* said it was 'a decided addition to the ornamental buildings of the town' and praised its facilities. The lending department, capable of holding over 5,000 volumes, a reading room, and a reference room were situated on the ground floor. There was a smoking room (for gentlemen!) with an adjoining recreation room for games such as chess, draughts, and whist on the first floor.

The local School Board, established following the Education Act of 1872, conducted a census of children in the town before assessing the requirements for the introduction of compulsory education. Although the population was increasing rapidly the existing schools were considered to be adequate for the foreseeable future. By 1881, however, they had become grossly overcrowded and so the Board decided to erect a school, later known as the Central, on Charlotte Street. Costing £6,800 and planned for 754 pupils (including 212 infants), it was opened on 12 September 1882. By the end of the nineteenth century it was so overcrowded that the Scotch Education Department withheld £90, a tenth of the total annual grant to the School Board, to emphasise its displeasure with the situation. The Board decided to remedy the overcrowding by building a school catering exclusively for the youngest pupils. Shown here – with part of the nearby Central School, with its distinctive tower, just visible on the extreme right – the Infant School was formally opened by Lord Saltoun on 18 September 1901, with a roll of 502 pupils. This freed accommodation in the Central School and so the Education Department refunded the £90. Two days before the opening, the School Board sanctioned the purchase of several items regarded as essential in a state-of-the-art infant school. These included a rocking-horse; four gutta percha balls; material for paper folding; an enamelled basin with a sponge attached to a cane for wiping pupils' slates (one to be provided in each room); four fireguards for the lowest infants' and babies' rooms; a coal scuttle for each room; fire-irons for the teachers' rooms; thermometers; a harmonium with a chair; pointers; a notice board to display the numbers present every day; a frame with glass for displaying the school timetable; pictures for the walls; and a table and a clock for the central hall.

Fraserburgh's first Academy was opened in Mid Street in August, 1870. Built and endowed by James Park, erstwhile clothier in Castle Street, it initially served its day and generation well but, from 1899 to 1903, HM Inspectors of Schools annually criticised its situation, accommodation, and equipment. In 1904, the Scotch Education Department condemned the Elementary schools in High Street and Broadsea and also warned the School Board that the Academy might lose its Higher Grade status if the required improvements were not made. The Board considered building a combined Elementary and Higher Grade School but decided to erect two schools. Dr Dunn, HM Chief Inspector of Schools, praised the Board for this decision when he formally opened the Higher Grade School (illustrated here, later called Fraserburgh Academy), on 8 June 1909. He also expressed the hope that other School Boards would come to Fraserburgh, 'as they would to a kind of intellectual Mecca', to obtain information and inspiration as to the best equipment and construction! The completion of the North Elementary, for 470 pupils, in College Bounds and the new Academy, for 400 pupils, in Dennyduff Road, brought the total expenditure on educational buildings in the town in the previous 30 years to £30,000.

It was generally acknowledged that Fraserburgh had been slow in modernising its herring fleet. This was graphically illustrated when William Norrie photographed the *Norseman* (BF1411) against a forest of masts belonging to local sailing drifters in Fraserburgh harbour. Prior to 1907 there were only four FR-registered steam drifters, none of them built locally; in the same period, there were fourteen registered in Banff, including the *Norseman*, which had been built and registered there in 1903. (The *Norseman* sprang a leak and foundered about six miles off Fraserburgh on 26 July 1912.) By 1907, it was generally agreed that the prosperity of the herring industry in Fraserburgh depended on steam drifters. Potential owners of new wooden boats were encouraged to have them built in local yards and the Harbour Commissioners were urged to lease land to enable the building yards to expand to cope with the increased demand.

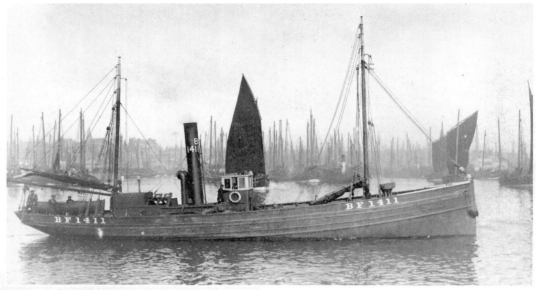

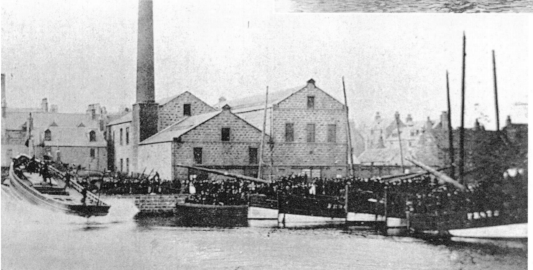

The first locally built steam drifter, the *Kinnaird* (FR205), left the stocks in Wilson Noble's yard, adjacent to the Balaclava Basin, on 27 February 1907. Part of the quay had to be chipped away before the launch, pictured here, could take place! Three days later, after a stone building was partly demolished to clear a path to the sea, the *Taits* (FR212), was launched from the Forbes yard at Sandhaven! On 20 March, the *Anchor of Hope* (FR214), built by the same firm, was manhandled 20 feet to be launched on the ways used for the *Taits*! No such heroic efforts were required when Scott & Yule launched the *Speedwell* (FR201) from their yard in Fraserburgh on 14 March. These three firms built twelve wooden steam drifters in 1907, some of them for other ports. Several vessels were purchased furth of Fraserburgh and so there were 27 steam-powered FR-registered drifters by the end of the year.

In order to cater for the rapidly increasing number of steam herring drifters based in the port for the summer herring fishery, the Harbour Commissioners embarked on the most ambitious part of their harbour improvement programme. From 1912 to 1914, over 400 men were employed in constructing a huge new basin with quays providing berthing and discharging facilities for about 230 boats (see pages 24 and 25). Stormy weather during the summer of 1912 destroyed a coffer dam and caused a costly interruption to the work. The rocks and mud excavated from the basin were used to extend the reclaimed area beyond the South Breakwater and to begin the formation of the promenade at the beach. Eventually, well behind schedule and significantly over budget, the new harbour was ceremonially opened on 27 July 1914. In the following week the First World War began. Before it ended, at least 89 locally registered steam drifters were requisitioned for war service; nine of them were lost.

Fraserburgh was *en fête* on Monday 27 July 1914. Uniformed Gordon Highlanders, Naval Reservists, and the Town Pipe Band added colour to the scene as the latest harbour extension was ceremonially opened. The official party walked in procession from the Town House to the Lifeboat Jetty where the principal guests boarded the drifter *George Walker* (FR 415), named after and partly owned by the oldest member of the Harbour Board; other guests boarded the paddle-tug *Blucher*. They sailed to the new harbour where a ribbon was stretched across the entrance. Accompanied by the Dundee Salvation Army Band, which was visiting the town, the crowds on the quays sang the 100th Psalm during a short service conducted by the minister from the West Parish Church. Lady Saltoun, acting on behalf of her husband, who was indisposed, then cut the ribbon.

After officially opening the new harbour, Lady Saltoun announced that it would 'hereafter be called the Faithlie Basin in remembrance of the ancient village of Faithlie, on the site of which the large and prosperous town of Fraserburgh has risen'. (In spite of this, years later, the fishing community often referred to the basin as the New Harbour.) Then the *George Walker* and the *Blucher*, both dressed overall, sailed into the new basin and berthed alongside one of the new jetties, where a decorated ceremonial arch had been erected. The guests disembarked and the official proceedings ended with a cake and wine banquet in the Town House. Next day, somewhat ironically, the first herrings to be discharged in the Faithlie Basin came from the hold of an old fashioned sailing drifter, the *Home Rule*. Herring buyers competed keenly for the honour of purchasing the inaugural landing and the price reached a spectacular 45 shillings a cran!

Taken from the guiding light at the outer end of the North Breakwater, this view was photographed when work on the most ambitious harbour extension (see page 21), between 1912 and 1914, was at an advanced stage. The Coastguard Houses (see page 39) are visible on the left at the southern end of Saltoun Place. Beyond the railway station, to the right of centre, is the South Church (built 1878–80), where the only relic of Fraserburgh University – the Moses Panel (see page 3) – can be seen. At the west end of Victoria Street, the spire of the West Church, built between

1876 and 1877, is visible beyond the five-storey tower of the Dalrymple Hall, dating from 1881. Adjacent to it is the Warld's End, originally the townhouse of the Gordons of Glenbuchat, which was recast to its present form in 1767. The first market, built 1899, for the sale of white fish by auction, is on the extreme right at harbour level.

The row of houses at the east end of the road to Strichen, near the junction with the main road to Aberdeen, was originally named St Modan's Gate, commemorating Fraserburgh's patron saint. In May 1901 the town council discussed minor improvements at this junction. After a new road across the Links was made, the possibility of upgrading the area was on the agenda again at a meeting in February 1902. It was proposed to feu a triangular area of ground from Lord Saltoun and then surface the roadways, form gravel footpaths kerbed with granite, and build retaining walls. Consideration was also given for 'an ashlar wall with granite cope and malleable iron railing, exactly similar to what was recently put round the New Infant School, to be built on the triangular piece of ground'. These plans did not come to fruition but a more ambitious series of improvements was carried out two years later. In March 1904 the town council agreed that the ground at the junction of the Strichen and Aberdeen turnpikes should be 'made into a street' with 'improvements and ornamentation'. The necessary ground was leased rent-free from Lord Saltoun and his factor approved the plans for 'the widening of the road to the North West corner of the West Link Park' and the erection of an ornamental gate, railing, and fountain, with one alteration. It was considered to be 'more in keeping with the crest of the Superior of the Burgh were the fountain surmounted by an ostrich instead of an eagle' (see page 28). St Modan's Gate was renamed Strichen Road soon after these improvements were completed.

A severe snowstorm hit the Fraserburgh district on the night of 27–28 December 1908. The town was inaccessible, except by sea, for nearly a week and supplies of bread were exhausted before main roads were reopened. Streets were impassable and wreaths reached the eaves of houses. The area near the junction of King Edward Street and Strichen Road was said to resemble 'the side of a Swiss hill in mid-winter'. This view of the snow-clearing work there was photographed on 30 December 1908, and appeared on a postcard franked in Fraserburgh on 2 January 1909! The height of the snow may be gauged in relation to the 15-foot sewer ventilator, the top which can be seen on the extreme right of the picture. It was one of six shafts installed in the town in 1902, in the hope that they would improve the sewage system and 'have a beneficial effect on the health of the burgh'. In November 1904 the burgh surveyor reported that they had been a benefit and so the town council approved the installation of another six shafts 'in congested areas and where sewers wind about'.

In January 1920 a committee was formed to arrange for a 'Memorial to Soldiers and Sailors belonging to Fraserburgh who fell in the war'. It was decided that it should be a monument paid for by public subscription. The Links, Saltoun Square, and two areas in the Bellslea Park were among the sites suggested. Alexander Carrick, an Edinburgh sculptor, was commissioned to design the monument and select the most suitable location for it. In October 1920 he reported that the best site was already occupied by the fountain at the junction of Strichen Road and Saltoun Place. He also said that, due to the backlog of work among the firms capable of casting the bronze figures and panels he had designed for the monument, the completion date would be three years hence. His report was accepted and so, as shown, the fountain was moved to its present site on Saltoun Place adjacent to the building which had been the burgh school from 1838 to 1882.

Alexander Carrick designed the monument to suit the site he had selected. Facing south-east to get as much light as possible, a bronze sculpture of a female figure restraining a soldier – allegorical for Justice Guiding Valour – stands on a granite pedestal with four bronze panels bearing the names of 411 men killed in the war. (Extra panels were added to commemorate those killed in the Second World War.)

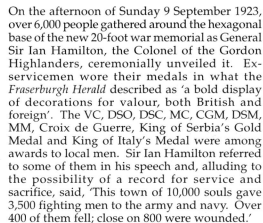

On the afternoon of Sunday 9 September 1923, over 6,000 people gathered around the hexagonal base of the new 20-foot war memorial as General Sir Ian Hamilton, the Colonel of the Gordon Highlanders, ceremonially unveiled it. Ex-servicemen wore their medals in what the *Fraserburgh Herald* described as 'a bold display of decorations for valour, both British and foreign'. The VC, DSO, DSC, MC, CGM, DSM, MM, Croix de Guerre, King of Serbia's Gold Medal and King of Italy's Medal were among awards to local men. Sir Ian Hamilton referred to some of them in his speech and, alluding to the possibility of a record for service and sacrifice, said, 'This town of 10,000 souls gave 3,500 fighting men to the army and navy. Over 400 of them fell; close on 800 were wounded.'

In the autumn of 1922, Fraserburgh Town Council decided to create work for about 50 of the local unemployed and, at the same time, increase the town's sporting facilities. The new amenities were opened for public use on 9 July 1923. They comprised a wooden pavilion, with an 18-hole putting green and a 6-rink bowling green on one side and four blaize tennis courts on the other. The facilities were laid out on the east side of the Aberdeen turnpike, between its junction with Strichen Road and the cricket pitch near the CPT factory. The pavilion housed changing rooms for players, a refreshment room, the superintendent's office, an equipment store, and toilets. An ornamental arch with the town's coat of arms and motto, *In God is all*, surmounted the entrance from the Links, where football and hockey pitches were being laid out in readiness for the winter season. The project was completed for under £5,000, including the cost of the wrought iron railings, which were bought at the displenish sale when the airship base at Lenabo was dismantled.

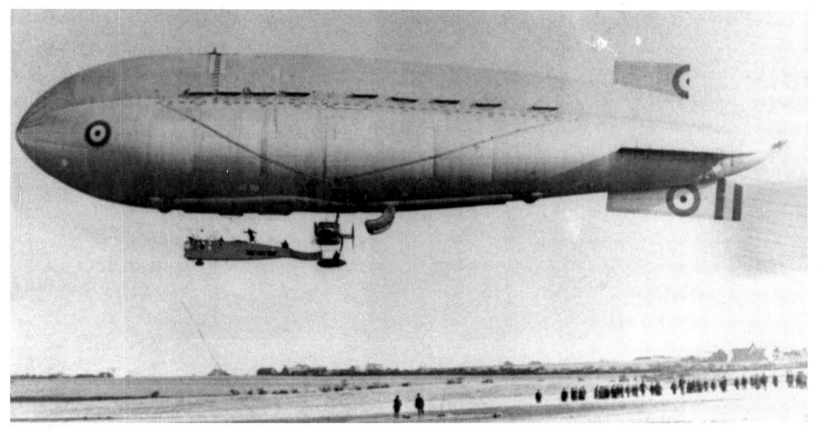

In 1916 the Admiralty established an airship base at Lenabo, about three miles from Longside, Aberdeenshire. Airships, able to stay on patrol for long periods, played a vital role in protecting shipping from attack by German submarines. When at full strength, there were three classes of airships stationed at Lenabo but the locals, who likened them to huge, fat sows, called them all 'Lenabo Soos' (in the Buchan dialect, a sow is known as a 'soo'.) A propeller, salvaged after a C class airship crashed into the sea, is on display in St John's Church, Longside. According to the accompanying plaque, it was driven by a 20 h.p. Renault engine. The North Sea (NS) class, shown here, was the biggest (262 feet long), fastest (with a maximum speed of 57½ m.p.h.), and could remain airborne for nearly 50 hours at a time in suitable flying conditions. An enclosed cabin, with cooking facilities heated by the exhaust gases from the engines, was suspended from the inflated envelope. The crew – captain, second pilot, two coxswains, two engineers, two wireless telegraph operators, and two gunners – worked a watch system. After the war ended the base was closed and, some years later, parts of two dismantled NS airships were among a wide variety of equipment, fittings, and furnishings sold at auction (see previous page).

The Consolidated Pneumatic Tool Company (CPT Co.), specialising in the manufacture of portable tools powered by compressed air, was formed in 1899 by the amalgamation of two independent companies, one operating in London and the other in Chippenham. Shortly afterwards, the directors of the new company (which had its head office in London although it was a fully-owned subsidiary of the Chicago Pneumatic Tool Co. in America) decided to build a factory in Britain. Archibald Maconochie, MP for East Aberdeenshire and founder of the Kinnaird Head Preserve Works, who had apparently been associated with the Chippenham works, offered to help them to find a suitable site. He arranged a visit to Fraserburgh, where they met Lord Saltoun and agreed to lease 50 acres on the southern out-

skirts of the town. Being an astute businessman and aware that Parliament had recently voted £300,000 for pneumatic tools for naval shipyards, Mr Maconochie recognised that this new and expanding industry would diversify the local economy, which was almost entirely based on fishing and its ancillary occupations, some of which were only seasonal. There was no local pool of skilled machine operatives, accustomed to working in an environment geared to mass production, as illustrated on the facing page. Nevertheless, he managed to persuade the directors of the CPT Co. to choose a site remote from essential materials and markets. With twenty years' experience as an employer in Fraserburgh, he presumably emphasised the virtuous work ethic of the Brochers, who would be receptive to training in the skills required in an industry at the cutting edge of technology. He would, of course, have also emphasised that the labour force was cheaper than in many other areas! Construction work continued from 1904 until the factory, with its distinctive octagonal chimney, went into full production in 1906, at which point the adjacent road was named Maconochie Road. An Edinburgh firm erected the structural steelwork while local contractors built the stonework in granite from quarries at Rora and New Pitsligo; material from the latter was used on the frontage on Maconochie Road. The state-of-the-art building was heated 'on the hot air system' while the 'saw-tooth roof', providing maximum light and ventilation to the machine and benchwork areas, was unique in Britain. Three automatic fireproof doors separated the machine room from the store, which was adjacent to the company's private railway siding linked to the line between Fraserburgh and Aberdeen. The factory aroused the interest of the cognoscenti. Travelling by railway, members of the Society of Mechanical Engineers, London, were taken 'right to the door', via the firm's private siding, when they visited the new 'Steel Works', as it was known locally, in 1907. 80 years later, long after the CPT Co. had become something of an institution in the town, it ceased production on 31 December 1987. Since then, various firms have occupied parts of the building.

Until 1914, production was concentrated on riveting and chipping hammers for shipyards, railway workshops, and heavy engineering contracts. Exports increased steadily and the company established overseas branch offices to maximise sales and facilitate distribution. During the First World War, with about 450 employees, the factory was engaged in armament production. After the war ended, tools for use in shipyards and railway workshops were produced in large quantities. From 1921 to 1924, however, the factory felt the effects of the depression and only a few workers and a skeleton managerial staff were employed. Recovery from the recession was helped by the development of specially designed rock drills, which were used extensively in important mining and tunnelling contracts; e.g. when setting a record for shaft sinking in South Africa. Drilling and riveting tools for aeroplane manufacture, tools for use on roadworks, and portable compressors were also developed. By the time the Toolies, as the factory had become known locally, was 30 years old, it is estimated to have contributed £1,000,000 to the local economy by way of wages paid. The pneumatic drills and hammers used in building the *Queen Mary* came almost exclusively from Fraserburgh and bridges in Sydney in Australia, at Lambeth in London, and on the Tyne were riveted entirely with CPT Co. tools. This picture shows the factory's automatic lathes.

In this view of the inspection room, note the posters publicising ongoing contracts and exhorting employees to buy goods from the relevant countries. As the variety and volume of the products multiplied, the inspection room played an increasingly important role in maintaining the high standard for which the company had gained an international reputation. Shortly before the Second World War began, the Toolies was one of only two factories subcontracted by Rolls Royce to make booster units for Merlin engines, which were used in Spitfire and Hurricane fighter planes. During the war the total workforce grew to about 2,400, of whom nearly half were women. Two sites previously used by fish processors, one in Albert Street and the other in Denmark Street, were converted to factory units as outstations of the Maconochie Road works. About 50,000 boosters for Rolls Royce and parts for 500 Bofors anti-aircraft guns were produced. Tools for shipbuilding and aircraft production were made at nearly three times the pre-war rate; the output of compressors was doubled; and sludge pumps, originally designed for draining flooded mines, were adapted for pumping oil from tankers damaged by enemy action.

After the Second World War began, members of the staff in the company's head office at 170 Piccadilly, London, were evacuated to two large country houses, Cairness and Crimonmogate, where they lived and worked within easy reach of Fraserburgh. Responding wholeheartedly to the wartime slogan 'Dig For Victory', they became partly self-sufficient with vegetable gardens, cows producing milk, and pigs being fattened! There were at least five air raids directed at the camouflaged Maconochie Road factory. On one occasion a bomb exploded within 40 yards of it; during another raid, an incendiary bomb penetrated the roof but did not ignite and was later discovered in a storage bin. The works had its own Anti-aircraft and Bomb Disposal Units; the latter was mobilised to help in the clearing-up operations in Aberdeen after the city was blitzed on 21 April 1943. Mr John Forbes, aircraft spotter at the factory, was awarded the George Medal after he rescued two girls who had strayed into a nearby beach minefield. John U. Vass, works manager, and John Strachan, who oversaw the production of the aero-engine units, were both created MBE for their contributions to the war effort. This picture shows a workshop containing precision grinding machines.

From its earliest days, the company adopted a positive approach to the welfare of its workers. About half of the original 50-acre site, across Maconochie Road from the factory, was eventually taken up by company houses built for employees. The writer of a contemporaneous account of the erection of the Steel Works (which had a bicycle store for the workers) was impressed by the provision of 'lavatory facilities, where employees could enjoy a refreshing wash after the labours of the day'. He also praised the opportunity that workers had been given to 'change into more dressy habiliments' and leave their damp working clothes overnight in ventilated lockers and find they were dried ready for wear next morning. By the 1920s, a committee of employees was overseeing the use of a clubroom – shown here on the top floor of the engineering shop – which housed a library and facilities for pastimes such as billiards, bowls, board games, music, and listening to the wireless. During the Second World War, the company helped to alleviate the domestic chores of their full-time female workers by employing six women, on a part-time basis, to do their shopping.

As the works expanded and the number of employees increased, it became the ambition of many local youths to serve an apprenticeship in the Toolies and the company developed a planned training scheme. In addition to on-the-job supervision in the various works departments, appropriate subjects – engineers' mathematics, for example – were available in local evening classes. In time, work schedules were amended and transport organised to allow employees to attend more advanced classes in Robert Gordon's Technical College, Aberdeen, with a view to acquiring Higher National qualifications. The firm also established a bursary to enable recipients to undertake three years' full-time study, at degree level, in Aberdeen. This staff development programme played its part in ensuring that the drawing office (illustrated here), where designs were continually revised to meet the specific requirements of customers, was always manned by competent personnel and so kept the factory among the world leaders in the production of pneumatic tools. It also meant that once they had acquired the appropriate qualifications, employees were more likely to seek to widen their horizons by finding employment elsewhere, as many of them did!

The export trade in cured herrings was at a low ebb in the early 1930s. The effects of the world recession were exacerbated by the uncertainties associated with Hitler's rise to power in Germany and by the Soviet Union's financial difficulties. After prolonged negotiations, however, the markets for cured herrings were reopened in both countries. Seen here on the quay prior to being loaded for Germany in 1933, this shipment established a new record as the largest cargo of cured herrings to leave Fraserburgh.

The record was short-lived. Able to carry 30,000 barrels, and by far the biggest vessel to berth in Fraserburgh, the Leningrad steamer *Sukhona* (shown entering the harbour), arrived on 27 October 1934. The *Fraserburgh Herald* reported, 'Berthing was a ticklish job, but she was manoeuvred into the Faithlie Basin (see page 21) without mishap'. Carrying the largest shipment of cured herrings from the port, 16,400 barrels for the Soviet government, she sailed on 31 October for Shetland to load a further 6,000 barrels.

Coastal life saving apparatus was based in Fraserburgh from 1854. In 1865 the Admiralty arranged a 99 year lease, from Lord Saltoun, of a site on Saltoun Place for the erection of the Admiralty Buildings, known later as the Coastguard Station or Coastguard Houses. Built in 1869, this provided accommodation for the life saving apparatus, a two-storey watch-room, a 'house' for the station officer, and six 'cottages' for his staff. (Lance-Cpl Charles Jarvis, awarded the first VC of the First World War for his bravery in action at Mons on 23 August 1914, was born here in March 1881, while his father was serving as a coastguard.) A Life Saving Apparatus (LSA) Company, including volunteers from the town and professional coastguards, was established in 1887; a similar company had been formed at the Coastguard Station at Rattray Head in 1865; and, in 1869, a company consisting entirely of volunteers was set up at Cairnbulg.

The volunteer-in-charge of the Cairnbulg LSA Company was on bad weather duty on Monday 27 February 1933. Soon after 10 p.m., he heard a distress signal from a ship aground at the north end of Whitelink Bay. He fired the conventional maroon (a very loud detonating firework) to call out the volunteers. On reaching Whitelink Bay, guided by a flare on the vessel's foredeck, they made two unsuccessful attempts to fire a rocket across the stricken boat (seen here after the storm had abated) and so bring the breeches buoy into operation. Arriving shortly before midnight, the Fraserburgh Company also failed to do so. It was pitch-dark, with heavy seas and a southerly gale and the Fraserburgh lifeboat was unable to approach the stranded boat, which, with no radio communication, was identified as the Granton trawler *North Queen* when a can bearing her name was washed ashore. After the Rattray Head Company arrived on the scene a line was successfully fired across the wreck, which had been driven inshore but was still some 200 yards from the beach. After another hour's struggle, with some of the volunteers up to their necks in the sea, the first ashore in the breeches buoy – by tradition, the cook – was injured as he was hauled face down across submerged rocks. The skipper, tenth and last off the ship, was pulled to the beach at 5 a.m.

The Fraserburgh Ship Repairing Co. paid £30 for the *North Queen* as she lay on the rocks at Whitelink Bay. 'Experts' said it was unlikely she could be towed off and repaired. However, the enterprising new owners, with improvised equipment and ad hoc methods took advantage of a particularly fine summer to prove the pundits wrong. At the top of a high tide on 6 September 1933, three herring drifters – *Mary Herd* (FR24), *Xmas Rose* (FR531), and *Alex Watt* (FR586) – pulled the *North Queen* into deep water. Pumps driven by temporary motor engines,

installed in the wreck by the salvors, kept the flow of water into the damaged vessel in check as she was towed to Fraserburgh. Seen here entering the harbour, with the *Mary Herd* alongside, she was safely beached near the inner end of the Lifeboat Jetty.

The starboard side of the *North Queen* was badly damaged, the stern post and propellor had gone, and the keel was broken. After being made completely seaworthy again, the trawler sailed from Fraserburgh on 9 September 1934 with a new identity; she had been renamed and registered in Aberdeen as *Fintry* (A135).

41

On 13 February 1934, while the *North Queen* was still undergoing extensive repairs, a special ceremony was held in the Dalrymple Hall, Fraserburgh. Captain Rashleigh, CBE, Chief Inspector of Coastguards, presented the Board of Trade Shield to the Cairnbulg, Fraserburgh, and Rattray Head Companies for their rescue of the trawler's crew. Awarded annually to the LSA Company in Great Britain or Northern Ireland which had performed the best wreck service of the year, this was the first time that three companies had shared the shield. The Fraserburgh Company is shown with its rocket launching apparatus and, on the right, the breeches buoy.

Back row: G. Bruce; G. Gray; G. Watt; Coastguard P. Inkson; Coastguard A. Hayman; W. Sim; A. Tait; J. Finlayson.

Front row: J. M'Ghee Buchan; G. Drake; B. Scott; Inspector W. R. Smailes (District Officer); Inspector W. Warnett (Station Officer); A. Anderson; J. Yule; T. Lawson; S. Drake.

Captain Rashleigh also highlighted the help given by people who were not members of the LSA Companies. Robert Third, a Cairnbulg shopkeeper, received special mention for forcing his car over the bents and training its headlights on the scene of the operations; the audience was told the companies had since been equipped with searchlights! A young teacher in Inverallochy School, George Flett, was also praised for his yeoman service. Still in his sports gear, he had come straight from playing badminton in the village hall to the scene of the rescue, where he helped to operate the breeches buoy whilst up to his chest in the sea. Note the instruction 'SIT IN BREECHES FACING SHORE' on the Cairnbulg Company's breeches buoy. This photograph shows members of the Cairnbulg LSA Company.

Back row: J. Stephen Jnr.; J. Stephen; J. May; (Mr W. R. Smailes, District Officer); (Captain A. L. Fletcher, RN, Inspector); J. Stephen; W. Cardno.
Middle row: A. Buchan; R. Duthie; W. Buchan; J. Duthie; G. Tait; J. Tait; A. Duthie; R. Cardno.
Front row: J. Greig; A. Whyte; W. Third; J. Summers, Volunteer in Charge; R. Stephen; A. Sutherland, A. Buchan.
Lying on ground: G. Cassie; N. Cromerty.

The LSA Companies were called out when the Finnish freighter *Anna* grounded at St Combs in December 1959. RNLI lifeboats were unable to approach the vessel and so the breeches buoy was the only means of rescue. There was no radio contact with the *Anna* but, in Morse by torchlight, the captain signalled that his crew would not leave the vessel until daylight. By then, the freighter had been driven to within 100 yards of the shore as shown in this view looking along Church Street, St Combs.

FINNISH VESSEL "ANNA" AGROUND AT ST COMBS.

Seventeen men were pulled to safety but the captain refused to abandon ship. The *Anna*'s owners sent a cable advising him to come ashore. It was delivered to him in a bottle in the breeches buoy and after 24 hours alone on the stricken vessel, he reluctantly complied with his employers' wishes. The *Anna* was a total loss; most of her deck-cargo was washed ashore and beachcombing became a lucrative pastime on the Buchan coast. Timber merchants in Leith and Grangemouth, consignees of the cargo, paid the salvage price for battens, which had been stacked beyond the high water mark and reported to the Receiver of Wrecks at Fraserburgh.

Three special trains, comprising 49 suitably adapted wagons, transported the personnel, horses, tents, and other paraphernalia when Col. W. F. Cody presented Buffalo Bill's Wild West and Congress of Rough Riders on the Fraserburgh Links on Tuesday 30 August 1904. In a typical publicity stunt, Buffalo Bill led his Red Indians to the South Pier where William Norrie photographed them. They then posed, as seen here, on the rocks at Kinnaird Head for another photograph. After a conducted tour of the Kinnaird Head Preserve Works, each of the party was presented with a tin of

Maconochie's canned herrings! The *Fraserburgh Herald* reported that some 19,000 spectators paid a total of over £1,500 to see the show, which was produced at a daily cost of £700. Most of this went to pay for the 600 loaves, 880 pounds of potatoes, 1,400 pounds of other vegetables, 25 hundredweights of meat, 600 bushels of oats, 6 tons of straw, and 6 tons of hay required by the 500 horses and 800 people who kept the show on the road.

In April 1904 a London periodical, *The King and His Navy and Army*, featured 'a curious little community of fishermen golfers at Inverallochy, near Fraserburgh'. Some of the members of Inverallochy Golf Club, founded in 1888, are pictured on their home course, where they had never lost an inter-club match. When Mr Maconochie, the local MP, arranged a match against the Edinburgh Burgess Club at Barnton, the fishermen were defeated, being unaccustomed to the turf on the fairways and the smooth greens. In spite of this, Mr Maconochie arranged a 10-a-side match to be played on 1 April 1905 at Royal St George's, Sandwich, between the fishermen and a team representing the House of Commons – including the Prime Minister, Mr A. J. Balfour. On arrival in London, the visitors were hospitably entertained and taken on a sightseeing tour. Next day, they practised at Sandwich but were ill at ease on the greens, which were like billiard tables compared to those on their own links. On match-day the MPs led by three matches to two at lunchtime, but the fishermen were whitewashed in the afternoon. Each fisherman was presented with a memento of the match – a golf club suitably inscribed by his opponent. This unique event is commemorated annually when teams of seniors from local golf clubs compete on Inverallochy golf course for the House of Commons Cup.

This print was published as a postcard entitled 'Mid-day meal in the harvest field, Fraserburgh'. The original photograph was taken during 'piece-time' on a hairst day in the Glebe, Aberdour, in 1889. At that time, harvesting was very labour intensive and the workers were allotted specific tasks. Cutting the standing crop with scythes was the work of the men; with one scythe in operation, it usually took 2–2½ days to harvest an acre. Women gathered the cut stalks into bundles ready for binding into sheaves; they also made the bands of straw with which the men tied the sheaves. The men set up the sheaves to dry, ten or so together in a stook, aligning them appropriately for the lie of the land and the prevailing wind. Once dried, the sheaves were 'led' – collected into stacks – to await threshing day.

J. A. Harvie-Brown, the internationally renowned naturalist from Dunipace, Larbert, wished to acquire a vessel, which, while useful for his fieldwork in the Scottish islands, would be sufficiently robust for a voyage to Arctic waters. Aware that several vessels had sailed from Fraserburgh for the Greenland whaling, he arranged for a boat to be built in the town. Named *Shiantelle* when launched in May 1887, with a mainsail measuring 342 square yards, she was capable of nine knots an hour. Before leaving on a voyage to the north and west of Scotland in June 1887, Harvie-Brown recruited William Norrie, who had recently established a studio on Cross Street, Fraserburgh, as the expedition's photographer. The *Shiantelle* was the last of at least 57 vessels, excluding local fishing boats, built by the family firm founded by John Webster in 1840. The firm had never built a whaling vessel but had double-hulled three boats, built elsewhere, to prepare them for the Greenland fishing. This experience stood them in good stead and meant that the *Shiantelle* was very sturdily built.

With William Norrie as photographer, Harvie-Brown led five very successful expeditions to the western and northern Scottish islands between 1887 and 1891. A year later, he sold the *Shiantelle* for £700 after she was involved in a collision off Oban, when her bowsprit passed right through the McBrayne passenger streamer, *Pioneer*.